Test Your Vocabulary – Book 1

Peter Watcyn-Jones

Illustrated by Sven Nordqvist

PENGUIN BOOKS

Penguin Books Ltd, Harmondsworth, Middlesex, England
Viking Penguin Inc., 40 West 23rd Street, New York, New York 10010, U.S.A.
Penguin Books Australia Ltd, Ringwood, Victoria, Australia
Penguin Books Canada Limited, 2801 John Street, Markham, Ontario, Canada L3R 1B4
Penguin Books (N.Z.) Ltd, 182–190 Wairau Road, Auckland 10, New Zealand

First published in Sweden by Kursverksamhetens förlag 1980
Published in Penguin Books 1985
Reprinted 1985, 1986, 1987

Text copyright © Peter Watcyn-Jones, 1980
Illustrations copyright © Sven Nordqvist, 1980
All rights reserved

Made and printed in Great Britain by
Hazell Watson & Viney Limited,
Member of the BPCC Group,
Aylesbury, Bucks
Set in Times

INTRODUCTION

Owing to the emphasis in recent years on functional and communicative approaches to language learning, many other important areas of the language have been neglected. One such area is vocabulary. This series is an attempt to remedy this situation not only by filling a real gap in the materials available but also by attempting to show that vocabulary learning can be just as much fun and just as stimulating as other activities. There are five books altogether in the series, ranging from Elementary level to Advanced. Each book contains fifty tests or exercises and, to facilitate self-study, a key is also included. Students using these books should find vocabulary learning both stimulating and enjoyable and, hopefully, start to develop a real sensitivity to the language.

Test Your Vocabulary – Book 1 is the second book in the series and is intended for elementary/lower intermediate students. There are approximately 700 words in the book arranged, where possible, into areas of vocabulary, for example, things in the home, clothes, jobs, holidays and festivals, shops and buildings, tools, and so on. In addition, there are fourteen picture tests which concentrate on everyday objects found at home and at work – things which the student ought to know the names of but rarely does since they seldom appear in conventional textbooks. Finally, there are tests on synonyms and antonyms, prepositions, choosing the most appropriate word, plus many more. As in all the books in this series, the techniques employed are very varied.

TO THE STUDENT

This book will help you to learn a lot of new English words. But in order for the new words to become "fixed" in your mind, you need to test yourself again and again. Here is one method you can use to help you learn the words:

1. Read through the instructions carefully for the test you are going to try. Then try the test, writing your answers **in pencil**.
2. When you have finished, check your answers and correct any mistakes you have made. Read through the test again, paying special attention to the words you didn't know or got wrong.
3. Try the test again five minutes later. You can do this either by covering up the words (for example, in the picture tests) or by asking a friend to test you. Repeat this until you can remember all the words.
4. **Rub out your answers**.
5. Try the test again the following day. (You should remember most of the words.)
6. Finally, plan to try the test at least twice again within the following month. After this most of the words will be "fixed" in your mind.

CONTENTS

1 Things in the home 1

Write the number of each drawing next to the correct word. (See example).

knife	10
vacuum cleaner	. . . . .
spoon	. . . . .
measuring jug	. . . . .
toaster	. . . . .
electric kettle	. . . . .
pair of scissors	. . . . .
fork	. . . . .
electric mixer	. . . . .
gravy jug	. . . . .

2 Synonyms – adjectives

Write down a synonym for each of the words on the left. Choose from the ones on the right. Number 1 has been done for you.

1 glad	....happy........	silent
2 nice	....	happy
3 wonderful	....	amusing
4 awful	....	boring
5 strange	....	rude
6 very big	....	inexpensive
7 optimistic	....	good-looking
8 funny	....	terrible
9 handsome	....	marvellous
10 dull	....	hopeful
11 impolite	....	simple
12 intelligent	....	huge
13 quiet	....	peculiar
14 easy	....	clever
15 cheap	....	pleasant

3 Countries and nationalities

Fill in the following crossword and see how many countries and nationalities you can remember.

DOWN

1 Aristotle was born in this country.
2 .... people love skiing.
3 These people make very good radios, television sets and stereos.
4 See crossword.
5 The flamenco is a typical .... dance.
6 One of the most well-known .... drinks is vodka.
7 Brigitte Bardot is ....
8 Britain was at war with this country from 1939—45.
9 A country where they eat a lot of spaghetti.
10 The .... football team lost 2—1 in the 1974 World Cup final.

ACROSS

1 This country is to the west of Spain.
2 One of the countries of Gt. Britain.
3 Hemingway's nationality.
4 This country has lots of mountains.
5 .... people drink a lot of tea.
6 The composer, Grieg, was ....
7 The capital of this country is Budapest.
8 These people eat a lot of rice.

4 Things in the home 2

Write the number of each drawing next to the correct word. (See example).

frying pan	. . . . .
grater	. . . . .
rolling pin	. . . . .
mincer	. . . . .
plate rack	. . . . .
saucepan	. . . . .
electric iron	. . . . .
casserole	. . . . .
kitchen scales	. . . . .
cruet	. . . . .
corkscrew	. .8. .

BS2

5 Quantities

Fill in the correct phrase under each drawing.

a tin of
a bottle of
a bar of
a packet of
a loaf of
a joint of
a roll of
a tube of
half a pound of
a dozen
a jar of
a box of

. . . . toothpaste

. . . . jam

. . . . soup

. . . . butter

. . . . eggs

. . . . meat

. . . . lemonade

. . . . matches

. . . . soap

. . . . bread

. . . . biscuits

. . . . film

6 Phrases 1

Fill in the missing words in the following drawings. Choose the phrases from the ones below:

a Oh, I hope not!

b It's a pleasure.

c The same to you.

d Very well, thank you.

e Congratulations!

f That's all right.

g Thank you.

h Yes, certainly.

i No, of course not.

j So do I.

7 Things in the home 3

Write the number of each drawing next to the correct word.

bathroom scales . . . . .
radiator . . . . .
table lamp . . . . .
fan . . . . .
tin opener . . . . .
hair dryer . . . . .
electric shaver . . . . .
pocket calculator . . . . .
ashtray . . . . .
filter coffee maker . . . . .

8 Guess their jobs

Read through the sentences and then write down which job each of the following people have.

1. MR GREEN 2. MISS EVANS 3. MR. BROWN 4. MRS WATKINS 5. MR WATSON

6. MRS SIMONS 7. MISS GEORGE 8. MR JONES 9. MR GIBSON 10. MISS KENT

1 This person cuts men's hair.
2 You go to this person when you have toothache.
3 You go to this person if you want a new pair of glasses.
4 This person looks after you when you are flying.
5 This person makes sure that no one parks their car in the wrong place, or parks somewhere for too long. Not many people like this person!
6 This person cuts and styles women's hair.
7 Before a house is built, this person draws the plans for it.
8 If something goes wrong with your pipes, wash basin or bath, you usually call for this person.
9 This person writes for a newspaper or magazine.
10 This person works in a library.

Mr Green is a b . . . .   Mrs Simons is a h. . . . .

Miss Evans is a d . . . .   Miss George is an a . . . .

Mr Brown is an o. . . . .   Mr Jones is a p. . . . .

Mrs Watkins is an a . . . .   Mr Gibson is a j . . . .

h . . . .   Miss Kent is a l . . . .

Mr Watson is a t. . . . .

w . . . .

9 Synonyms – verbs

Write down a synonym for each of the words on the left. Choose from the ones on the right. Number 1 has been done for you.

1 talk	_speak_	depart
2 love	....	help
3 hate	....	adore
4 fall	....	mend
5 phone	....	receive
6 swim	....	allow
7 leave	....	comprehend
8 let	....	ring
9 ask	....	loathe
10 cry	....	require
11 assist	....	weep
12 get	....	speak
13 need	....	inquire
14 understand	....	stumble
15 repair	....	bathe

10 Name the sport

Fill in the following crossword. Each answer is a different sport.

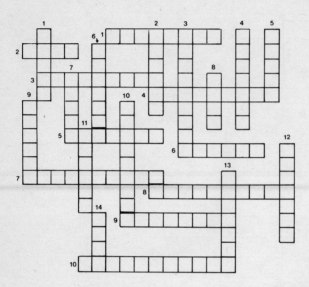

DOWN

1 Played with a ball this shape
2 Björn Borg's sport.
3 This includes things like running, jumping etc.
4 An English game foreigners find difficulty in understanding.
5 Team game – played outdoors on ice.
6 Popular winter sport.
7 English pub game.
8 Hole in one!
9 A violent sport.
10 Done in water.
11 It is dangerous to attack someone who takes part in this sport.
12 In this sport you roll something along the ice.
13 Sport on two wheels.
14 Played on horseback. Prince Charles is quite good at it!

ACROSS

1 Favourite sport in England.
2 Self-defence. A gentler form of 11 down.
3 A game similar to tennis.
4 Canada's national sport.
5 Indoor sport on ice.
6 Very fast indoor game for 2 players.
7 Both Olga Korbut and Nelly Kim won gold medals at the Olympic Games in this sport.
8 V...........
9 Could it be called football using hands instead of feet?
10 A very fast and dangerous sport.

11 Tools, etc

Write the number of each drawing next to the correct word.

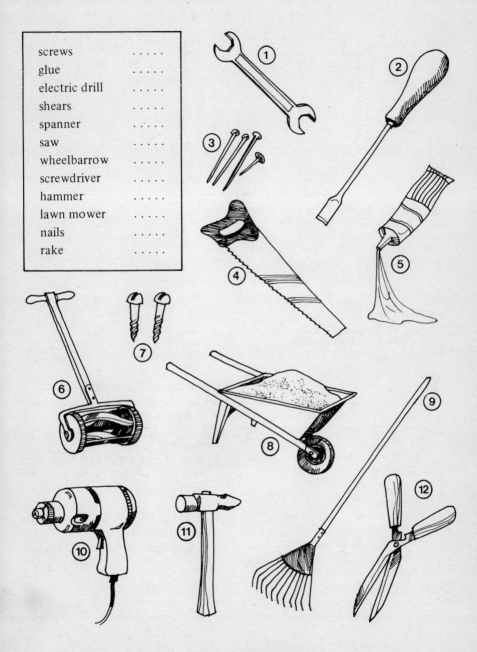

screws . . . . .
glue . . . . .
electric drill . . . . .
shears . . . . .
spanner . . . . .
saw . . . . .
wheelbarrow . . . . .
screwdriver . . . . .
hammer . . . . .
lawn mower . . . . .
nails . . . . .
rake . . . . .

12 Opposites – verbs

Write down the opposite of each of the words on the left. Choose from the ones on the right. Number 1 has been done for you.

1 start	......*finish*.........	arrive
2 go in	....	hate
3 find	....	come out
4 catch	....	forget
5 stop	....	fail
6 succeed	....	save
7 raise	....	demolish
8 buy	....	lose
9 depart	....	mend
10 spend	....	continue
11 love	....	drop
12 accept	....	finish
13 break	....	lower
14 construct	....	reject
15 remember	....	sell

13 Newspaper misprints

In each of the following extracts from a newspaper there is a misprint (usually a word) which completely changes the meaning of the sentence. Write down the word which is wrong and also write down which word should have been used instead.

	Misprint	Correct word
1 A thief went into the changing room at Hastings United football club. Honey was taken from the pockets of five players.	*Honey*	*Money*
2 The final practice for the children's concert will be hell on Saturday afternoon between 2.00 and 2.30.		
3 Woman wanted to share fat with another.		
4 The man was holding a gin as he entered the bank.		
5 As well as the usual prizes, over 50 swimming certificates were presented. The school choir sank during the evening.		
6 Mr Davies who was on the boat deck, ran to the rails and threw a lifeboat to the drowning man.		
7 Detectives kept a witch on the house for two weeks.		
8 Lady required for 12 hours per week to clean small officers at Station Road, Oxford.		
9 Arsenal are hoping their new centre forward will be fat enough to play on Saturday against Manchester United.		
10 All the bridesmaids wore red noses.		

14 Prepositions 1

Fill in the missing prepositions in the following sentences.

1 I'm very interested .... football.
   a of   b in   c for

2 Would you like some wine .... the meal?
   a to   b for   c with

3 I'll be back .... an hour.
   a in   b for   c after

4 Is John married .... Eva?
   a by   b to   c with

5 I've been learning English .... two years.
   a for   b in   c since

6 I went to Stockholm .... air.
   a with   b on   c by

7 I bought my son a bicycle .... his birthday.
   a for   b to   c in

8 I was in the army .... the War.
   a under   b for   c during

9 He lives .... the corner of Green Street and Links Road.
   a by   b at   c with

10 Don't speak .... him now; he is not feeling very well.
   a at   b to   c with

11 Why are you .... such a bad mood today?
   a in   b on   c at

12 Where are you going .... your holidays?
   a to   b under   c for

15 Shops and buildings

On the following map are ten shops or buildings.
Read through the information below and write down the names of the different shops or buildings.

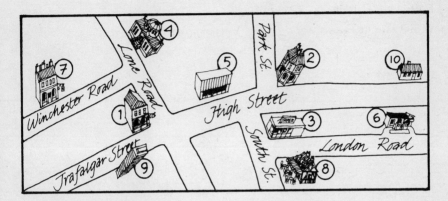

Building number 4 has lots of books in it.

The building in Trafalgar Street has 15 floors.

You can buy a bottle of wine to take home somewhere in Winchester Road.

The building at the corner of Park Street and High Street sells medicine.

Building number 9 is divided into flats.

If you are hungry, you can always go to South Street.

The Browns live in building number 10.

The building at the corner of Lone Road and Trafalgar Street is where you can have a drink with friends.

You can buy stamps at building number 5.

Mrs Brown always shops for food in the building at the corner of South Street and London Road. It's cheaper there!

The Browns live in a house with only one floor.

If you want petrol, go to the building in London Road.

Number 1 is a . . . .   Number 6 is a . . . .

Number 2 is a . . . .   Number 7 is an . . . .

Number 3 is a . . . .   Number 8 is a . . . .

Number 4 is a . . . .   Number 9 is a . . . .

Number 5 is a . . . .   Number 10 is a . . . .

16 Furniture and fittings 1

Write the number of each drawing next to the correct word.

stool	. . . . .
mirror	. . . . .
Welsh dresser	. . . . .
dressing table	. . . . .
standard lamp	. . . . .
dish washer	. . . . .
roller blind	. . . . .
venetian blind	. . . . .
light switch	. . . . .
wall socket	. . . . .

17 Choose the word 1

Write in the missing word in the following sentences.

1 When you buy something, you are usually given a ....
   a recipe   b receipt   c bill

2 You must .... for at least two hours a day if you want to play the piano well.
   a train   b practice   c practise

3 Most banks will .... people money to buy a house.
   a lend   b give   c borrow

4 I wonder if you can .... me to play the guitar?
   a assist   b teach   c learn

5 I always feel very nervous when I have to .... a speech.
   a make   b perform   c do

6 We had a very .... time in London last summer.
   a fun   b nice   c funny

7 Would you .... this letter to the Post Office, please?
   a send   b take   c bring

8 The .... in the north of Sweden is really beautiful.
   a scenery   b nature   c view

9 My wife has a .... job at a chemist's.
   a half-time   b spare-time   c part-time

10 I saw a very good .... advertised in the paper this week.
   a job   b work   c occupation

11 If you put money in the bank, you get about 8% ....
   a increase   b interest   c rent

12 When I was in Denmark, I .... a boat for a few days.
   a hired   b rented   c leased

18 Food

Fill in the following crossword.

		1 B				
2		A				
		3 C				
4		O				
	5	N				
	6	A				
	7	N				
	8	D				
	9	E				
10		G				
	11	G				
12		S				

1 The meat we get from a cow.
2 The meat we get from a calf.
3 A vegetable.
4 The meat we get from a sheep.
5 A fruit.
6 Another sort of meat.
7 These vegetables make you cry!
8 A bird, often served with orange sauce.
9 The most popular drink in England.
10 Fruit. Also a colour.
11 It makes things taste sweet.
12 English people often eat fish and ....

19 Road signs

Here are 12 road signs found in England. Write the correct words under each sign.

Maximum speed limit	No entry	No overtaking
Slippery road	Keep left	No waiting
One-way traffic	Width limit	Pass either side
Two-way traffic straight ahead	Height limit	No through road

20 Parts of the body

Write the numbers 1–30 next to the correct word.

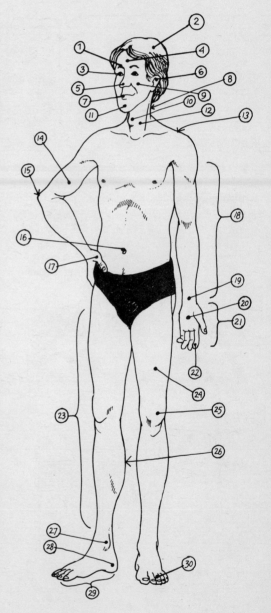

hand	. . . . .
ankle	. . . . .
navel	. . . . .
eyebrow	. . . . .
chin	. . . . .
leg	. . . . .
wrist	. . . . .
hair	. . . . .
toe	. . . . .
eye	. . . . .
finger	. . . . .
knee	. . . . .
cheek	. . . . .
forehead	. . . . .
elbow	. . . . .
ear	. . . . .
heel	. . . . .
mouth	. . . . .
nose	. . . . .
foot	. . . . .
shoulder	. . . . .
neck	. . . . .
thumb	. . . . .
palm	. . . . .
throat	. . . . .
thigh	. . . . .
arm	. . . . .
calf	. . . . .
biceps	. . . . .
Adam's apple	. . . . .

21 Furniture and fittings 2

Write the number of each drawing next to the correct word.

shelf	. . . . .
armchair	. . . . .
chair	. . . . .
footstool	. . . . .
pouffe	. . . . .
pelmet	. . . . .
chest of drawers	. . . . .
wash basin	. . . . .
sink unit	. . . . .
bathroom cabinet	. . . . .
cupboard	. . . . .
spotlight	. . . . .

22 Missing words – people's characteristics

Put the following words in the correct sentence.

friendly	bad-tempered	shy	patient
generous	talkative	lazy	reliable
jealous	imaginative		

1 My wife is always .... in the mornings. She gets angry at the slightest thing.

2 The thing I like about John is that he is so .... If he tells you he'll do something, then he always does it.

3 My husband is so .... He's always buying me things.

4 Paul's new girlfriend is very ...., isn't she? She hardly says a word and always looks down at the floor when she talks to you.

5 Don't ask Janina to dance — at least not if Clive, her husband, is looking. He gets so ...., you know.

6 Our new teacher is so .... If we don't understand something she goes over it again and again until we do.

7 I think English people are so .... They'll always talk to you and try to help you even if you've never met them before.

8 Pam loves to talk a lot, doesn't she? In fact, I don't think I've ever met anyone quite as .... as her.

9 Paul's wife never does any housework, even though she doesn't go out to work. I really can't understand how anyone can be so ...., can you?

10 I wish my husband were as .... as Janet's. Do you know he just makes up stories to read to the children at bedtime without the least effort. It's wonderful, isn't it?

B59

23 Prepositions 2

Look at the plan of the boat, then fill in the missing prepositions in the sentence.

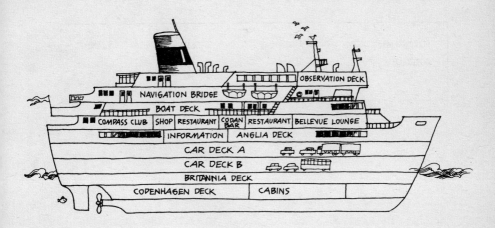

1 The Britannia Deck is .... Car Deck B.

2 The restaurant is .... the shop and the Codan Bar.

3 The Bellevue Lounge is .... the restaurant.

4 There are cabins .... the Copenhagen Deck.

5 The Observation Deck is .... the Navigation Bridge.

6 You can find your cabin number .... the Reception desk.

7 You can have a meal .... the restaurant.

8 There are steps leading .... the Observation Deck.

9 There's a rail running .... the side of the Boat Deck.

10 You have to go past the shop if you go .... the Compass Club .... the restaurant.

24 Classifications

Write one name for each of the following groups. Before starting, look at the example.

1 pig, dog, sheep, lion

2 iron, silver, copper, lead

3 shirt, tie, blouse, dress

4 wren, pigeon, thrush, eagle

5 knife, fork, soup spoon, teaspoon

6 beech, poplar, oak, willow

7 cousin, uncle, nephew, aunt

8 maize, wheat, barley, oats

9 plate, cup, saucer, bowl

10 trout, salmon, herring, cod

11 bee, ant, fly, beetle

12 motorbike, car, tram, lorry

13 crocus, daffodil, snowdrop, primrose

14 beer, milk, water, paraffin

15 saucepan, frying pan, grater, baking dish

16 violin, cello, trumpet, guitar

17 pounds, marks, yen, crowns

18 butcher, baker, salesman, tailor

19 snake, lizard, crocodile, chameleon

20 table, sofa, bookcase, chair

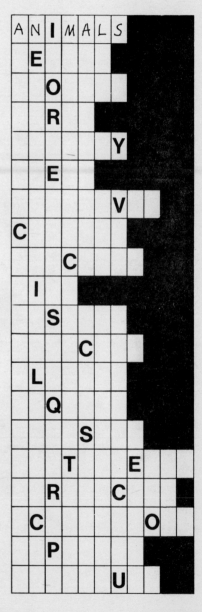

25 Complete the dialogue

In the following dialogue, the part of Jennifer has been left out. Put in the words she speaks in the right order from the phrases below.

- A bar of Lux, please.
- And a dozen eggs, please.
- Haven't you?
- A packet of crisps, please. And a bar of soap.
- Standard, please.
- Yes, please.
- Thank you. Cheerio.
- Hello, Mr Davies. I'd like half a pound of butter, please.
- And a tin of pears, please.
- No, just one more thing — a pound of cheese, please.
- All right. I'll take a tin of peaches, then.

Mr Davies: Hello, Jenny. What can I do for you?

Jennifer: ....

Mr Davies: Yes. Anything else?

Jennifer: ....

Mr Davies: Large or standard?

Jennifer: ....

Mr Davies: Here you are.

Jennifer: ....

Mr Davies: Oh, I'm afraid we haven't got any pears left.

Jennifer: ....

Mr Davies: No, but we've got lots of peaches.

Jennifer: ....

Mr Davies: Right you are. Anything else?

Jennifer: ....

Mr Davies: Yes. Now, what sort of soap do you want?

Jennifer: ....

Mr Davies: Right. Is that all?

Jennifer: ....

Mr Davies: Cheddar?

Jennifer: ....

Mr Davies: Right, then, let's see now... That's £1.51 altogether please, Jenny.

(Jennifer hands him £2)

Thank you. And 49p change.

Jennifer: ....

Mr Davies: Cheerio, love.

26 Clothes 1

Write the number of each drawing next to the correct word.

polo-neck jumper	. . . . .
jacket	. . . . .
panties	. . . . .
bra	. . . . .
suit	. . . . .
a pair of socks	. . . . .
underpants	. . . . .
shawl	. . . . .
belt	. . . . .
tie	. . . . .
skirt	. . . . .
shirt	. . . . .

27 Choose the word 2

Write in the missing word in each of the following sentences.

1 I had to keep my son home from school today because he had a ....
.... of 38.
   a fever   b headache   c temperature

2 Is there anything .... you'd like me to get you?
   a else   b more   c extra

3 I like going to England in the summer because it gives me a ....
.... to speak English.
   a chance   b case   c possibility

4 When we were in Spain last year we .... at a marvellous ho-
tel overlooking the beach.
   a stayed   b stopped   c lived

5 My sister lives .... London.
   a nearly   b near   c in the near of

6 Does your husband ever offer to do the .... ?
   a washing-up   b discussing   c dishing

7 The doctor gave her a .... for some medicine.
   a recipe   b statement   c prescription

8 When a fire broke out in the Louvre, at least twenty ....
paintings were destroyed, including two by Picasso.
   a worthless   b priceless   c valueless

9 There is a lot of talk nowadays about .... Rights.
   a Humane   b Manly   c Human

10 I usually .... up at 7 o'clock in the morning.
   a get   b awake   c go

11 The psychiatrist asked his patient to .... down on the couch.
   a lay   b sit   c lie

12 The new musical was a great success. The .... loved it.
   a audience   b spectators   c crowd

28 School report

Read through the following School report and try to write in the names of the subjects. Look at the example first.

HASTINGS COMPREHENSIVE SCHOOL		SCHOOL REPORT

Pupil's name: **Joanna Steele** Class: **4B**

SUBJECT	GRADE	TEACHER'S REMARKS
ENGLISH	C+	Quite good, but her spelling needs to improve.
	B	Good. Her holiday in Paris has certainly helped her a lot.
	C-	Needs to work harder - especially at map reading.
	A	An excellent pupil. Very interested in the subject and her project on "Roman Britain" was the best I have ever read.
	D+	Poor. Still uses her fingers to count!
	C	Fair. A lot to learn but seems to enjoy doing experiments.
	B+	Always tries hard and is becoming an excellent tennis player.
	E	Very poor. Hates the subject - especially singing.
	C+	Quite good. Likes drawing teachers!
	B	A good pupil. Regularly does the readings at Morning Assembly.

31

29 Phrases 2

Fill in the missing words in the following drawings. Choose the phrase from the ones below.

a Yes, please do.
b Oh, I hope not.
c Oh, what a pity!
d Yes, that's right.
e Nice to see you, too.

f Yes, I'd be glad to.
g Ah well, it can't be helped.
h Yes, it is rather.
i Oh, how awful.
j Yes, not too bad, thanks.

33

30 Clothes 2

Write the number of each drawing next to the correct word.

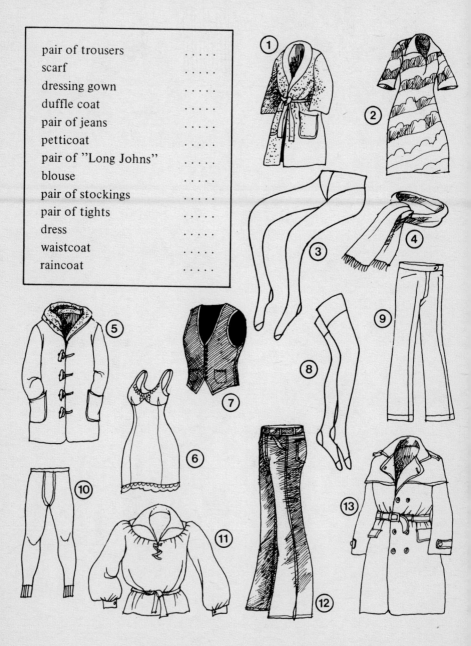

pair of trousers	. . . . .
scarf	. . . . .
dressing gown	. . . . .
duffle coat	. . . . .
pair of jeans	. . . . .
petticoat	. . . . .
pair of "Long Johns"	. . . . .
blouse	. . . . .
pair of stockings	. . . . .
pair of tights	. . . . .
dress	. . . . .
waistcoat	. . . . .
raincoat	. . . . .

31 Word association

Underline two of the words on the right which are associated with or are part of the word on the left. Number 1 has been done for you.

1	TREE	brim, <u>trunk</u>, car, <u>climb</u>, cabbage
2	HOUSE	laugh, attic, forest, tongue, brick
3	BICYCLE	speak, saddle, town, pump, green
4	ORCHESTRA	go, needle, conductor, score, break
5	CHRISTMAS	pastime, decorations, lose, mistletoe, salmon
6	FOOTBALL	mole, corner, umpire, hornet, penalty
7	WEDDING	bride, storm, confetti, soap, blink
8	CAR	run, basket, clutch, boot, head
9	WAR	fight, cream, tank, apple, sincere
10	FLOWER	wren, petal, clean, buttercup, suggest
11	SCHOOL	brown, examination, dinner, offer, lesson
12	SLEEP	calm, nightmare, sheet, tongue, cushion
13	CHURCH	congregation, cough, aisle, feet, money
14	SHOE	snore, lace, heel, sit, height
15	BOOK	leaf, side, title, sheet, paperback
16	GOLF	tea, green, stick, birdie, cod
17	ENGLAND	light, Thames, **garlic**, pub, **Edinburgh**
18	FACE	heel, grin, writing, cheeks, ankle
19	TELEPHONE	switch, lure, dial, ramble, receiver
20	OFFICE	typewriter, lose, rabbit, file, perm

32 Cartoons

In the following cartoons, the captions (i.e. the words that go with a cartoon) have got mixed up so that each cartoon has been printed with the wrong caption under it. Work out the correct caption for each cartoon.

Cartoon	Correct caption	Cartoon	Correct caption
1	....	6	....
2	....	7	....
3	....	8	....
4	....	9	....
5	....	10	....

33 Puzzle it out

Here are five words:

CABBAGE   BANANA   CARROT   STRAWBERRY   EGG

Read through the following dialogue and try to work out which words the above are used instead of (e.g. if you think the word "egg" is used instead of "the" you write "Egg means the" etc.)

A: Excuse me, do you **cabbage** children?
B: No, I'm afraid I **banana**.
A: Oh, **carrot**'s a pity.
B: Why do you say **carrot**?
A: Because everyone should **cabbage** children.
B: Why?
A: Well, **strawberry**'s only natural.
B: I disagree. I **egg carrot** there are far too many children in the world already and I certainly **banana** want to add to the numbers.
A: **Carrot**'s a strange way to **egg**.
B: Is **strawberry**? I **egg strawberry**'s the only sensible way to look at things.
A: Well, I certainly want to **cabbage** at least four children.
B: I **egg carrot**'s a very selfish attitude to take.
A: I **banana** care! **Carrot**'s what I'm going to do.
B: Well – go ahead – **cabbage** all those children but **banana** try to tell me to **cabbage** any.
A: **Banana** worry, **carrot**'s the last thing I'd **egg** of doing.
B: I'm glad to hear **strawberry**.

CABBAGE means . . . .   BANANA means . . . .
CARROT means . . . .   STRAWBERRY means . . . .
EGG means . . . .

34 Fruit and vegetables

Write the number of each drawing next to the correct word.

pineapple	. . . . .
grapes	. . . . .
raspberry	. . . . .
celery	. . . . .
cucumber	. . . . .
lemon	. . . . .
corn cob	. . . . .
beetroot	. . . . .
cabbage	. . . . .
mushrooms	. . . . .
carrot	. . . . .
water melon	. . . . .
strawberry	. . . . .
cherry	. . . . .
peanuts	. . . . .
radishes	. . . . .

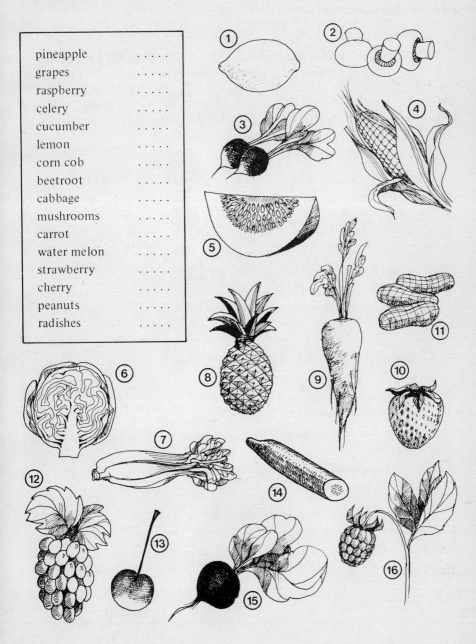

35 Synonyms – more adjectives

Write down a synonym for each of the words on the left. Choose from the ones on the right. Number 1 has been done for you.

1 sad	...... *unhappy*	evil
2 amusing	....	thrilling
3 wicked	....	dear
4 hard-working	....	unattractive
5 stubborn	....	witty
6 rich	....	furious
7 curious	....	wealthy
8 boring	....	dreadful
9 polite	....	industrious
10 expensive	....	uninteresting
11 angry	....	reserved
12 exciting	....	well-mannered
13 terrible	....	inquisitive
14 shy	....	unhappy
15 ugly	....	obstinate

36 Holidays and festivals

Fill in the following crossword.

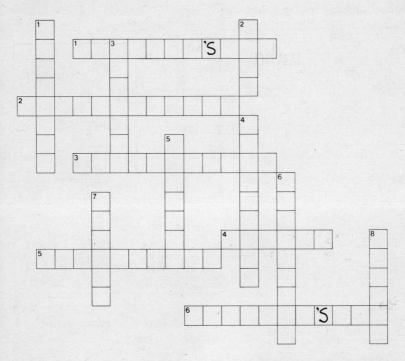

DOWN

1 Everyone has one of these days every year.
2 A .... Holiday is a special non-religious public holiday in Britain. There are usually three of these every year.
3 A religious festival in May.
4 British people call April 1st ....'s Day.
5 Most people like to relax at the ....
6 A time in Britain when people buy a lot of presents.
7 The day in the week when people go to church.
8 A religious festival in March/April.

ACROSS

1 The day when many people promise to try and better themselves by, for example, giving up smoking. (3 words)
2 The name for December 24th. (2 words)
3 I always forget our wedding ....
4 December 26th is called ...... day.
5 The day Christ was crucified. (2 words)
6 The name for December 31st. (3 words)

37 Places to live

Write the number of each drawing next to the correct word.

bungalow	. . . . .
tent	. . . . .
detached house	. . . . .
caravan	. . . . .
block of flats	. . . . .
castle	. . . . .
hotel	. . . . .
semi-detached house	. . . . .
lighthouse	. . . . .
windmill	. . . . .
cottage	. . . . .
palace	. . . . .
country house/mansion	. . . . .
terraced house	. . . . .
houseboat	. . . . .

38 Match up the pairs

Fill in the missing words in the following drawings.

reader
teacher
client
policeman
bride
patient
child
employer
tennis player
dummy
guest
shopkeeper

. . . . and thief

doctor and . . . .

writer and . . . .

. . . . and employee

host and . . . .

. . . . and pupil

44

.... and customer   parent and ....

lawyer and .... and opponent

ventriloquist and .... and groom

39 More jobs

Read through the sentences and then write down which job each of the following people have.

1. MRS SOUTH 2. MR HOPE 3. MISS BESWICK 4. MRS SHARK 5. MR GABB

6. MRS ADLER 7. MISS WOOD 8. MR GREY 9. MR SELLERS 10. MR RIGBY

1 This person is the head of a company.
2 You meet this person when you go to church.
3 You often see this person in plays on television.
4 You go to this person when you want to buy or sell a house.
5 This person helps run the country.
6 This person is called in to examine and report on the accounts of a company.
7 This person makes tables, chairs, doors, etc.
8 This person makes drawings in an office — often a new design or product.
9 He sells anything from a car to a paint brush. He usually travels a lot.
10 You can phone for this person if your house or flat is on fire.

Mrs South is a m............. d................ Mrs Adler is an a................................

Mr Hope is a c.................................... Miss Wood is a c................................

Miss Beswick is an a.............................. Mr Grey is a d.....................................

Mrs Shark is an e............. a................. Mr Sellers is a s............. r...................

Mr Gabb is a p................................... Mr Rigby is a f...................................

40 Prepositions 3

Put in the missing prepositions in the following sentences.

1 My wife has just been .... Spain.
   a to   b at   c in

2 That's really typical .... John. He says he'll come but he never turns up.
   a for   b of   c to

3 I've know him .... many years now.
   a for   b since   c in

4 I must be home .... 11.30 at the latest.
   a on   b by   c at

5 My children are really looking forward .... Christmas.
   a against   b at   c to

6 Do you usually have a holiday .... Easter?
   a at   b on   c for

7 I haven't seen John .... he got married.
   a until   b since   c before

8 What time do you usually get up .... the mornings?
   a on   b at   c in

9 My son's really afraid .... dogs.
   a of   b for   c with

10 I'm afraid I'm not very good .... English.
   a in   b with   c at

11 See you .... 4 o'clock, then.
   a on   b at   c in

12 There's no point .... saving nowadays, is there?
   a to   b with   c in

48

41 Choose the word 3

Write in the missing word in each of the following sentences.

1 .... have you been learning English?
  a For how long time   b How long   c How long time

2 I got married .... years ago.
  a for two   b in two   c two

3 What with inflation and everything, there's just no ....
saving nowadays.
  a idea to   b point in   c meaning to

4 You've got it all wrong, Jan. That wasn't ....
  a what I meant   b my meaning   c my purpose

5 I'm sorry but I didn't have .... to post the letters.
  a time enough   b enough with time   c enough time

6 Good morning. I .... see the manager, please.
  a will   b want to   c wish

7 Did you have .... in England last summer?
  a a nice time   b a funny time   c it very nice

8 I'm sorry, but I haven't .... today.
  a read my lesson   b done my lesson   c done my homework

9 I must remember to fill in my tax .... this week.
  a return   b declaration   c brochure

10 I thought Joanna said she .... spend the weekend with
her parents.
  a was going to   b should   c will

11 I hate doing the .... – especially cleaning the windows.
  a homework   b housework   c jobs

12 These shoes don't .... They're much too big.
  a suit   b pass   c fit

42 Bits and pieces 1

Write the number of each drawing next to the correct word.

paintbrush	. . . . .
safety pin	. . . . .
ruler	. . . . .
sewing machine	. . . . .
pencil sharpener	. . . . .
typewriter	. . . . .
paper clip	. . . . .
rubber	. . . . .
stapler	. . . . .
nib	. . . . .
punch	. . . . .
drawing pin	. . . . .
fountain pen	. . . . .
propelling pencil	. . . . .
ink	. . . . .

43 Missing words – parts of a house

Put the following words into the sentences below.

upstairs	double glazing	chimney	dining room
sitting room	French windows	letter-box	hall
skylight	downstairs	cellar	gutter
landing	attic	porch	central heating

1 A house consists of two floors — .... and ....
   ....

2 Smoke comes out of a ....

3 The room under a house is called the ....

4 The pipe at the bottom of the roof to carry away rainwater is called the ....
   ....

5 You eat in the ....

6 The space under the roof, often used for storing boxes, etc. is called the ....
   ....

7 Most families relax and watch television in the ....

8 A window which opens out onto the roof is called a ....

9 The postman delivers letters through the ....

10 Most modern houses have .... instead of
   open fires.

11 The space inside the front door (usually near the stairs) is called the ....

12 In modern houses, the windows are made up of two panes of glass instead
   of just one. This is called ....

13 The space at the top of the stairs is called the ....

14 Doors made of glass which usually open out onto the garden are called ......
   ....

15 In some houses, there is a covered space before you go through the front
   door. This is called the ....

44 Out of doors

Rearrange the letters to find out the names of the things in the following drawing.

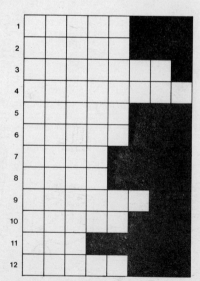

1	R	E	T	S	E
2	E	D	L	F	I
3	R	R	O	T	C	T	A
4	U	I	N	A	N	M	T	O
5	U	C	O	L	D
6	D	E	G	H	E
7	H	T	P	A
8	T	A	G	E
9	R	E	G	B	I	D
10	I	V	R	R	E
11	C	W	O
12	C	N	F	E	E

BS19

45 Bits and pieces 2

Write the number of each drawing next to the correct word.

rubber band	. . . . .
biro/ballpoint pen	. . . . .
lighter	. . . . .
hook	. . . . .
plug	. . . . .
tap	. . . . .
penknife	. . . . .
torch	. . . . .
date stamp	. . . . .
paper-fastener	. . . . .
envelope	. . . . .
toothbrush	. . . . .
dice	. . . . .
button	. . . . .
funnel	. . . . .

46 Opposites – more adjectives

Write down the opposite of each of the words on the left. Choose from the ones on the right. Number 1 has been done for you.

1 strong	..... _weak_	depressed
2 generous	....	noisy
3 exciting	....	lazy
4 innocent	....	mean
5 quiet	....	poor
6 simple	....	smooth
7 hard-working	....	sober
8 careful	....	boring
9 deep	....	attractive
10 rough	....	complicated
11 sharp	....	weak
12 wealthy	....	careless
13 ugly	....	shallow
14 happy	....	guilty
15 drunk	....	blunt

47 British and American English

Write down the missing British or American words. Look at the example first.

AMERICAN ENGLISH   BRITISH ENGLISH

1 sidewalk   .....pavement.....

2 .... taxi

3 apartment   ....

4 .... underground

5 apartment building   ....

6 .... petrol

7 candy   ....

8 .... shop

9 drugstore

10 .... autumn

11 movie

12 .... lift

13 railroad

14 .... tram

15 parking lot

48 A family tree

Look at the following family tree and then fill in the missing words in the sentences below. Look at the example first.

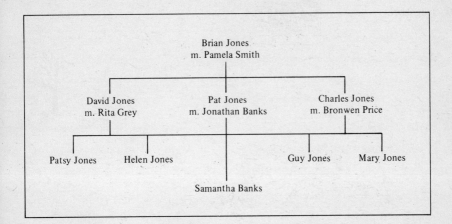

1 Brian is David's .... *father*.....................

2 Patsy and Samantha are ....

3 Charles is Pat's ....

4 Bronwen is Guy's ....

5 Pamela is Helen's ....

6 Rita is David's ....

7 Jonathan is Patsy's ....

8 Charles is Jonathan's ....

9 Pamela is Bronwen's ....

10 Rita is Mary's ....

11 Jonathan is Pat's ....

12 Guy and Mary are Brian's ....

13 Brian is Bronwen's ....

14 Patsy is Helen's ....

15 Jonathan is Brian's ....

16 Guy is David's ....

17 Guy is Bronwen's ....

18 Pat and Jonathan are Samantha's ....

19 Mary is Rita's ....

20 Rita is Brian's ....

49 Who uses what

Complete the sentences below by choosing a suitable word from the ones on the right. (Use each word once only).

1 A crash helmet is used by	a shop assistant
2 A whistle is used by.	a teacher
3 A typewriter is used by	a golfer
4 A palette is used by.	a businessman
5 Pins are used by.	a motorcyclist
6 A blackboard is used by	a referee
7 A chisel is used by.	a policeman
8 A tripod is used by	a doctor
9 A microscope is used by	a conductor
10 A stethoscope is used by	an artist
11 A rifle is used by	a camper
12 A till is used by	a dressmaker
13 An anvil is used by	a scientist
14 Handcuffs are used by.	a soldier
15 A sleeping bag is used by.	a secretary
16 A tee is used by.	a fireman
17 A wheelbarrow is used by	a blacksmith
18 A music stand is used by	a photographer
19 A ladder is used by	a gardener
20 A briefcase is used by	a carpenter

50 Bits and pieces 3

Write the number of each drawing next to the correct word.

protractor	. . . . .
bracelet	. . . . .
plant	. . . . .
needle	. . . . .
hook and eye	. . . . .
candlestick	. . . . .
compass	. . . . .
set-square	. . . . .
stepladder	. . . . .
bucket	. . . . .
padlock	. . . . .
zip	. . . . .
press stud	. . . . .
pins	. . . . .
cufflinks	. . . . .

Answers

TEST 1

knife	10
vacuum cleaner	6
spoon	9
measuring jug	8
toaster	7
electric kettle	5
pair of scissors	2
fork	4
electric mixer	3
gravy jug	1

TEST 2

1 happy
2 pleasant
3 marvellous
4 terrible
5 peculiar
6 huge
7 hopeful
8 amusing
9 good-looking
10 boring
11 rude
12 clever
13 silent
14 simple
15 inexpensive

TEST 3

Down
1 Greece
2 Austrian
3 Japanese
4 Swedish
5 Spanish
6 Russian
7 French
8 Germany
9 Italy
10 Dutch

Across
1 Portugal
2 Wales

3 American
4 Switzerland
5 English
6 Norwegian
7 Hungary
8 Chinese

TEST 4

frying pan	10
grater	2
rolling pin	5
mincer	1
plate rack	6
saucepan	3
electric iron	4
casserole	11
kitchen scales	7
cruet	9
corkscrew	8

TEST 5

a tube of toothpaste
a jar of jam
a tin of soup
half a pound of butter
a bottle of lemonade
a dozen eggs
a joint of meat
a loaf of bread
a box of matches
a bar of soap
a packet of biscuits
a roll of film

TEST 6

1 d
2 b
3 i
4 f
5 j
6 a
7 e
8 g
9 c
10 h

TEST 7

bathroom scales	7
radiator	4
table lamp	9
fan	6
tin opener	10
hair dryer	1
electric shaver	5
pocket calculator	3
ashtray	8
filter coffee maker	2

TEST 8

Mr Green is a barber.
Miss Evans is a dentist.
Mr Brown is an optician.
Mrs Watkins is an air hostess.
Mr Watson is a traffic warden.
Mrs Simons is a hairdresser.
Miss George is an architect.
Mr Jones is a plumber.
Mr Gibson is a journalist.
Miss Kent is a librarian.

TEST 9

1 speak
2 adore
3 loathe
4 stumble
5 ring
6 bathe
7 depart
8 allow
9 inquire
10 weep
11 help
12 receive
13 require
14 comprehend
15 mend

TEST 10

Down
1 rugby
2 tennis
3 athletics
4 cricket
5 bandy
6 skiing
7 darts
8 golf
9 boxing
10 swimming
11 karate
12 curling
13 cycling
14 polo

Across
1 football
2 judo
3 badminton
4 ice hockey
5 skating
6 squash
7 gymnastics
8 volleyball
9 handball
10 motor racing

TEST 11

screws   7
glue   5
electric drill   10
shears   12
spanner   1
saw   4
wheelbarrow   8
screwdriver   2
hammer   11
lawn mover   6
nails   3
rake   9

TEST 12

1 finish
2 come out
3 lose
4 drop
5 continue
6 fail
7 lower
8 sell
9 arrive
10 save
11 hate
12 reject
13 mend
14 demolish
15 forget

TEST 13

1	Honey	Money
2	hell	held
3	fat	flat
4	gin	gun
5	sank	sang
6	lifeboat	lifebelt
7	witch	watch
8	officers	offices
9	fat	fit
10	noses	roses

TEST 14

1 b
2 c
3 a
4 b
5 a
6 c
7 a
8 c
9 b
10 b
11 a
12 c

TEST 15

1 pub
2 chemist's
3 supermarket
4 library
5 post office
6 filling-station (garage)
7 off-licence
8 restaurant
9 block of flats
10 bungalow

TEST 16

stool   3
mirror   6
Welsh dresser   10
dressing table   4
standard lamp   8
dish washer   5
roller blind   1
venetian blind   9
light switch   7
wall socket   2

TEST 17

1 b
2 c
3 a
4 b
5 a
6 b
7 b
8 a
9 c
10 a
11 b
12 a

TEST 18

1 beef
2 veal
3 carrot
4 mutton
5 banana
6 lamb

7   onions
8   duck
9   tea
10 orange
11 sugar
12 chips

TEST 19

1   One-way traffic
2   Slippery road
3   Maximum speed limit
4   Height limit
5   No through road
6   Two-way traffic
    straight ahead
7   No entry
8   Keep left
9   No waiting
10 Pass either side
11 No overtaking
12 Width limit

TEST 20

hand	21
ankle	27
navel	16
eyebrow	1
chin	11
leg	23
wrist	19
hair	2
toe	30
eye	3
finger	22
knee	25
cheek	9
forehead	4
elbow	15
ear	6
heel	28
mouth	7
nose	5
foot	29
shoulder	13
neck	8
thumb	17
palm	20
throat	12
thigh	24

arm	18
calf	26
biceps	14
Adam's apple	10

TEST 21

shelf	8
armchair	7
chair	12
footstool	6
pouffe	2
pelmet	5
chest of drawers	3
wash basin	9
sink unit	11
bathroom cabinet	1
cupboard	10
spotlight	4

TEST 22

1   bad-tempered
2   reliable
3   generous
4   shy
5   jealous
6   patient
7   friendly
8   talkative
9   lazy
10 imaginative

TEST 23

1   below
2   between
3   next to
4   on
5   above
6   at
7   in/at
8   up to
9   along
10 from ... to

TEST 24

1   animals
2   metals
3   clothes
4   birds
5   cutlery
6   trees
7   relatives
8   cereals
9   crockery
10 fish
11 insects
12 vehicles
13 flowers
14 liquids
15 utensils
16 instruments
17 currencies
18 occupations
19 reptiles
20 furniture

TEST 25

Jennifer's part:

– Hello, Mr Davies. I'd like
half a pound of butter,
please.
– And a dozen eggs, please.
– Standard, please.
– And a tin of pears, please.
– Haven't you?
– All right. I'll take a tin of
peaches, then.
– A packet of crisps, please.
And a bar of soap.
– A bar of Lux, please.
– No, just one more thing –
a pound of cheese, please.
– Yes, please.
– Thank you. Cheerio.

TEST 26

polo-neck jumper	8
jacket	5
panties	12
bra	1
suit	7

a pair of socks	3
underpants	11
shawl	6
belt	2
tie	9
skirt	4
shirt	10

TEST 27

1	c
2	a
3	a
4	a
5	b
6	a
7	c
8	b
9	c
10	a
11	c
12	a

TEST 28

English
French
Geography
History
Maths/Mathematics
Science (Physics/Chemistry/
    Biology)
Games
Music
Art
Religion

TEST 29

1	g
2	e
3	j
4	a
5	h
6	c
7	f
8	b
9	d
10	i

TEST 30

pair of trousers	9
scarf	4
dressing gown	1
duffle coat	5
pair of jeans	12
petticoat	6
pair of "Long Johns"	10
blouse	11
pair of stockings	8
pair of tights	3
dress	2
waistcoat	7
raincoat	13

TEST 31

1	trunk, climb
2	attic, brick
3	saddle, pump
4	conductor, score
5	decorations, mistletoe
6	corner, penalty
7	bride, confetti
8	clutch, boot
9	fight, tank
10	petal, buttercup
11	examination, lesson
12	nightmare, sheet
13	congregation, aisle
14	lace, heel
15	title, paperback
16	green, birdie
17	Thames, pub
18	grin, cheeks
19	dial, receiver
20	typewriter, file

TEST 32

1	7
2	6
3	9
4	8
5	10
6	3
7	2
8	4
9	1
10	5

TEST 33

Cabbage means have
Banana means don't (do not)
Carrot means that
Strawberry means it
Egg means think

TEST 34

pineapple	8
grapes	12
raspberry	16
celery	7
cucumber	14
lemon	1
corn cob	4
beetroot	15
cabbage	6
mushrooms	2
carrot	9
water melon	5
strawberry	10
cherry	13
peanuts	11
radishes	3

TEST 35

1	unhappy
2	witty
3	evil
4	industrious
5	obstinate
6	wealthy
7	inquisitive
8	uninteresting
9	well-mannered
10	dear
11	furious
12	thrilling
13	dreadful
14	reserved
15	unattractive

TEST 36

Down
1 Birthday
2 Bank
3 Whitsun
4 April Fool
5 Weekend
6 Christmas
7 Sunday
8 Easter

Across
1 New Year's Day
2 Christmas Eve
3 Anniversary
4 Boxing
5 Good Friday
6 New Year's Eve

TEST 37

bungalow	3
tent	6
detached house	5
caravan	9
block of flats	1
castle	4
hotel	13
semi-detached house	12
lighthouse	7
windmill	2
cottage	15
palace	11
countryhouse/mansion	14
terraced house	8
houseboat	10

TEST 38

policeman and thief
doctor and patient
writer and reader
employer and employee
host and guest
teacher and pupil
shopkeeper and customer
parent and child
lawyer and client
tennis player and opponent
ventriloquist and dummy
bride and groom

TEST 39

Mrs South is a managing
  director
Mr Hope is a clergyman
Miss Beswick is an actress
Mrs Shark is an estate
  agent
Mr Gabb is a politician
Mrs Adler is an auditor
Miss Wood is a carpenter
Mr Grey is a draughtsman
Mr Sellers is a sales represen-
  tative
Mr Rigby is a fireman

TEST 40

1	a
2	b
3	a
4	b
5	c
6	a
7	b
8	c
9	a
10	c
11	b
12	c

(Note: (a) rather than (c) in
number 1 since "been" is
understood to mean the
same as the past perfect tense
of the verb "to go" in the
sence of to go and come back
or to visit.)

TEST 41

1	b
2	c
3	b
4	a
5	c
6	b
7	a
8	c
9	a
10	a
11	b
12	c

TEST 42

paintbrush	8
safety pin	5
ruler	12
sewing machine	10
pencil sharpener	15
typewriter	1
paper clip	4
rubber	9
stapler	13
nib	2
punch	14
drawing pin	6
fountain pen	3
propelling pencil	11
ink	7

TEST 43

1	upstairs – downstairs
2	chimney
3	cellar
4	gutter
5	dining room
6	attic
7	sitting room
8	skylight
9	letter-box
10	central heating
11	hall
12	double glazing
13	landing
14	French windows
15	porch

TEST 44

1	trees
2	field
3	tractor
4	mountain
5	cloud
6	hedge
7	path
8	gate
9	bridge
10	river
11	cow
12	fence

TEST 45

rubber band	3
biro/ballpoint pen	9
lighter	13
hook	2
plug	14
tap	10
penknife	6
torch	12
date stamp	7
paper-fastener	4
envelope	1
toothbrush	8
dice	11
button	15
funnel	5

TEST 46

1 weak
2 mean
3 boring
4 guilty
5 noisy
6 complicated
7 lazy
8 careless
9 shallow
10 smooth
11 blunt
12 poor
13 attractive
14 depressed
15 sober

TEST 47

1 pavement
2 cab
3 flat
4 subway
5 block of flats
6 gasoline
7 sweets
8 store
9 chemist's
10 Fall
11 film
12 elevator
13 railway
14 streetcar
15 car park

TEST 48

1 father
2 cousins
3 brother
4 mother
5 grandmother
6 wife
7 uncle
8 brother-in-law
9 mother-in-law
10 aunt
11 husband
12 grandchildren
13 father-in-law
14 sister
15 son-in-law
16 nephew
17 son
18 parents
19 niece
20 daughter-in-law

TEST 49

1 a motorcyclist
2 a referee
3 a secretary
4 an artist
5 a dressmaker
6 a teacher
7 a carpenter
8 a photographer
9 a scientist
10 a doctor
11 a soldier
12 a shop assistant
13 a blacksmith
14 a policeman
15 a camper
16 a golfer
17 a gardener
18 a conductor
19 a fireman
20 a businessman

TEST 50

protractor	5
bracelet	9
plant	11
needle	15
hook and eye	6
candlestick	13
compass	1
set square	12
stepladder	6
bucket	14
padlock	7
zip	10
press stud	4
pins	2
cufflinks	8